COME
THIRSTY

WORKBOOK

Receive What Your Soul Longs For

COME
THIRSTY

WORKBOOK

Receive What Your Soul Longs For

Based on the Book by

MAX LUCADO

NELSON REFERENCE & ELECTRONIC
A Division of Thomas Nelson Publishers
Since 1798

www.thomasnelson.com

Published by Thomas Nelson, Inc., P.O. Box 141000, Nashville, Tennessee, 37214.

Unless otherwise indicated, all Scripture quotations are from The Holy Bible: New Century Version (NCV). Copyright © 1987, 1988, 1991 by W Publishing Group, a Division of Thomas Nelson, Inc. Used by permission. All rights reserved.

Scripture quotations marked "NKJV" are taken from the New King James Version®. Copyright © 1979, 1980, 1982, 1990 by Thomas Nelson, Inc. All rights reserved.

Library of Congress Cataloging-in-Publication Data is available.

ISBN 1-4185-0027-5

Printed in the United States of America.

1 2 3 4 5 — 08 07 06 05 04

TABLE OF CONTENTS

"WHOEVER DRINKS OF THE
WATER THAT I SHALL GIVE
HIM WILL NEVER THIRST. BUT
THE WATER THAT I SHALL GIVE
HIM WILL BECOME IN HIM A
FOUNTAIN OF WATER SPRINGING
UP INTO EVERLASTING LIFE."

—John 4:14 NKJV

COME THIRSTY READING PLAN

Week 1

♦ Read the Introduction of *Come Thirsty*. As you read through "Meaghan," her story will sound strangely familiar. As this introduction unfolds, we discover a young woman who is thirsting for something real.

♦ Read Chapter 1 of *Come Thirsty*: "The Dehydrated Heart"—Unless we are drinking deeply at the well of God's supply, our hearts become dehydrated—dry, depleted, parched, and weak.

Week 2

♦ Chapter 2: "Sin Vaccination"—We were all born with a terminal disease—hopelessly infected by sin. See how God made a way for us to live disease free.

♦ Chapter 3: "When Grace Goes Deep"—Grace is a gift of God. Take a look at what happens when you try to put conditions on the grace of God. Grace is what defines us.

♦ Chapter 4: "When Death Becomes Birth"—Don't allow the dread of death to take away your joy of living.

♦ Chapter 5: "With Heart Headed Home"—We live caught between what is and what will be. Our hearts are longing for heaven, and every day that passes brings us closer to home.

Week 3

♦ Chapter 6: "Hope for Tuckered Town"—Some of us try to live our Christian lives completely in our own power. God offers hope for us when the effort wears us down.

♦ Chapter 7: "Waiting for Power"—Before we move forward, sometimes God asks us to wait … and pray.

♦ Chapter 8: "God's Body Glove"—The Holy Spirit works with us and through us, hand in glove.

♦ Chapter 9: "It's Not Up to You"—God paid too high a price for you to leave you unguarded. The Holy Spirit reminds us of our place in God's heart and comes to our aid in times of weakness.

Week 4

♦ Chapter 10: "In God We (Nearly) Trust"—We know that God knows what's best. We know that we don't. We also know that God cares, so we can trust him.

♦ Chapter 11: "Worry? You Don't Have To"—Worry changes nothing, and only shows that we aren't trusting God to do as he promised.

♦ Chapter 12: "Angels Watching Over You"—When you accept God's lordship in your life, you can be assured that many mighty angels will guard you in all your ways.

♦ Chapter 13: "With God as Your Guardian"—God guards those who turn to him.

Week 5

Prayer of the Thirsty

Lord, I come thirsty. I come to drink, to receive. I receive Your work on the cross and in Your resurrection. My sins are pardoned and my death is defeated. I receive Your energy. Empowered by Your Holy Spirit, I can do all things through Christ who gives me strength. I receive Your lordship. I belong to You. Nothing comes to me that hasn't passed through You. And I receive Your love. Nothing can separate me from Your love. Amen.

INTRODUCTION

Who are we? Busy people. Burdened people. Burned-out people. Strained, stressed, and stretched people, longing for refreshment. These are all symptoms of a dryness deep within. A need. A thirsting. Deprive your soul of spiritual water and it will tell you. Dehydrated hearts send desperate messages. Snarling tempers. Waves of worry. Whispers of guilt and fear. Hopelessness. Sleeplessness. Loneliness. Resentment. Irritability. Insecurity. But God doesn't want us to live like this.

Like the woman at the well, we must recognize our need for living water. Our hearts are parched, dry, dehydrated. We need moisture, a swallow of water, a long, quenching drink. And where do we find water for the soul? "If anyone thirsts, let him come to Me and drink. He who believes in Me, as the Scripture has said, out of his heart will flow rivers of living water" (John 7:37, 38 NKJV). Jesus invites: *Are your insides starting to shrivel?* Drink me. What H_2O can do for your body, Jesus can do for your heart. Come and see what the Lord can do in your heart! Come ready to receive the refreshment your soul longs for. Come, and come thirsty.

W-E-L-L

Receive Christ's Work on the cross.

Receive the Energy of his Spirit.

Receive his Lordship over your life.

Receive his unending, unfailing Love.

WEEK 1

THIRSTING AFTER RIGHTEOUSNESS

*"Blessed are those who hunger
and thirst for righteousness,
for they shall be filled."*

— Matthew 5:6 NKJV

Introduction

Have you ever been in the mood for ... *something* ... to eat? You've got the munchies, and you're looking for a snack. The only problem is that you're not quite sure what will satisfy your craving. Something salty? Something sweet? Something chewy? Something crunchy? It's hard to put your finger on what's driving you to rummage through the pantry. Nothing looks good, so you slam through the cupboards and poke around in the back of the fridge.

Our souls are not so different. We get a restless yearning for ... *something*. Our hearts are hungry. We are driven by a deep thirst. And so we cast about for something to satisfy our need. If we do not nourish our soul, it grows weak and weary. Deprived of sustenance, we become strained, stretched, and stressed. Scripture compares this desperate need with thirst. Are you thirsty?

> *"YOU GAVE THEM BREAD FROM HEAVEN FOR THEIR HUNGER, AND BROUGHT THEM WATER OUT OF THE ROCK FOR THEIR THIRST."*
>
> — Nehemiah 9:15 NKJV

1. Remember the children of Israel, wandering in the wilderness for forty years. They understood what it meant to be hungry and thirsty. "Hungry and thirsty, their soul fainted in them" (Ps. 107:5 NKJV). How does Isaiah 29:8 describe the hunger and thirst of men?

   "When a _____ man dreams, and look—he _____; but he _____, and his soul is still _____; or as when a _____ man dreams, and look—he _____; but he _____, and indeed he is _____, and his soul still _____." (NKJV)

2. Yet God provided for the physical needs of those who called upon him for relief. The people's dehydrated bodies longed for water, and that is just what God supplied. Match up these promises for refreshment with their texts.

____ Nehemiah 9:15   a. God didn't withhold the water from the thirsty.

____ Nehemiah 9:20   b. When God led in deserts, they didn't go thirsty.

____ Isaiah 41:17   c. Everyone who thirsts, come to the waters.

____ Isaiah 48:21   d. You brought them water out of the rock.

____ Isaiah 49:10   e. God has mercy, and leads by springs of water.

____ Isaiah 55:1   f. The needy seek water; their tongues fail for thirst.

"DEPRIVE YOUR BODY OF NECESSARY FLUID, AND YOUR BODY WILL TELL YOU. DEPRIVE YOUR SOUL OF SPIRITUAL WATER AND YOUR SOUL WILL TELL YOU."

God supplies our physical needs, sometimes in miraculous ways. Yet there are times when that doesn't feel like enough. "You have planted much, but you harvest little. You eat, but you do not become full. You drink, but you are still thirsty. You put on clothes, but you are not warm enough. You earn money, but then you lose it all as if you had put it into a purse full of holes" (Hag. 1:6 NCV). We have food to eat and water to drink, but they do not satisfy the longing that pervades our soul. We are thirsty, but for what? Where should we turn for relief?

3. Unfortunately, too many try to quench that restless hunger and nagging thirst with things that cannot satisfy. What does Paul say will be the end of those who pursue their appetites for earthly things, according to Philippians 3:19?

> *"BLESSED ARE THOSE WHO HUNGER AND THIRST FOR RIGHTEOUSNESS, FOR THEY SHALL BE FILLED."*
>
> —Matthew 5:6 NKJV

Jesus told his followers, "Blessed are you who hunger now, for you shall be filled" (Luke 6:21 NKJV). What a wonderful promise! But moments later, he turned this statement upside down. "Woe to you who are full, for you shall hunger" (Luke 6:25 NKJV). Consider this. Those who are satisfied with what the world has to offer no longer hunger and thirst after spiritual things. They opted for a shortcut. They settled for instant gratification. Those of us who continue to thirst after the living water only Jesus can supply will rely upon him right on into eternity. Our hunger will be satisfied in the very presence of God.

4. David understood the longing of his heart. He knew exactly what he was thirsty for.

   ♦ According to Psalm 42:2, what did David thirst for?

♦ To what did David compare his longing in
Psalm 143:6?

♦ What did David do, in an effort to assuage
his longing for God, according to Psalm 63:1?

5. So what should we be hungering for? What
should we be thirsting after? Jesus tells us in
Matthew 5:6.

There's no denying the urgency of our thirst. We
should heed it. We should drink. But when seeking to
quench our thirsty hearts, we must be certain to drink
good water. There can be no substitutes. If you are
indeed thirsting after righteousness, then the Lord
urges you to drink, and drink deeply.

6. Jesus tells us, "Seek first the kingdom of God
and His righteousness" (Matt. 6:33 NKJV). So,
what is righteousness? Match up these passages,
which give us a little overview.

_____ Psalm 11:7   a. The heavens declare his righteousness.

_____ Proverbs 11:19   b. The Sun of Righteousness will arise.

_____ Psalm 48:10   c. The LORD is righteous. He loves righteousness.

_____ Psalm 50:6   d. God has given us a robe of righteousness.

_____ Psalm 65:5   e. God works awesome deeds in righteousness.

_____ Psalm 119:172   f. Righteousness leads to life.

_____ Isaiah 61:10   g. He will be called: the LORD our righteousness.

_____ Jeremiah 23:6   h. God's right hand is full of righteousness.

_____ Malachi 4:2   i. All of God's commandments are righteousness.

Our first tendency in seeking righteousness is to try to *do* something. But the Lord is not asking us to do anything. We are called upon to receive what he has provided. "Not by works of righteousness which we have done, but according to His mercy He saved us" (Titus 3:5 NKJV).

"HE SHALL BRING FORTH YOUR RIGHTEOUSNESS AS THE LIGHT, AND YOUR JUSTICE AS THE NOONDAY."

—Psalm 37:6 NKJV

7. We need to cultivate a hunger and a thirst for righteousness, but we cannot achieve a righteous and godly life without divine assistance.

   ◆ What does God give to us, according to Psalm 24:5?

   ◆ God doesn't leave us to fend for ourselves. What does Psalm 23:3 say he will do for us?

   ◆ What glorious promise do we find in Psalm 37:6?

"NOW I AM RIGHT WITH GOD, NOT BECAUSE I FOLLOWED THE LAW, BUT BECAUSE I BELIEVED IN CHRIST. GOD USES MY FAITH TO MAKE ME RIGHT WITH HIM."

—Philippians 3:9 NCV

8. Throughout the New Testament, we are told that righteousness and right living are only possible by the grace of God. All we need to do is believe. Paul assures us that it is by faith that we are made righteous.

Romans 10:10: "We _____ with our _____; and so we are _____ _____ with God. And we use our mouths to say that we _____, and so we are _____." (NCV)

2 Corinthians 5:21: "He made Him who _____ no _____ to be _____ for us, that we might _____ the _____ of God in Him." (NKJV)

Ephesians 4:23, 24: "You were taught to be _____ _____ in your _____, to become a _____ _____. That _____ _____ is made to be _____ _____— made to be truly _____ and _____."
(NCV)

"IN ORDER FOR JESUS TO DO WHAT WATER DOES, YOU MUST LET HIM GO WHERE WATER GOES. DEEP, DEEP INSIDE."

Philippians 3:9: "Not having my own

_____, which is from the

law, but that which is through _____

in _____, the _____

which is from _____ by _____."

(NKJV)

There is some danger that a gift so freely given can be taken too much for granted. We can become numb to our thirst for a time. We can sink into apathy and lethargy. Scripture uses hunger and thirst to convey a sense of urgency. We are dependent upon God. We cannot live without him. We need him. In order to keep those truths before us, we must cultivate our appetite for righteousness. Stir up your hunger. Heed your thirst. Drink, and keep on drinking!

9. Do we hunger and thirst after righteousness? Yes! So what *can* we do about it? Pursue it!

♦ What does Paul urge his son in the faith to pursue in 1 Timothy 6:11?

♦ What did Jesus do in order to make our pursuit possible, according to 1 Peter 2:24?

♦ Where can we turn for help in our pursuit, according to 2 Timothy 3:16?

10. Jesus is the Source of everything we need. He calls to everyone, urging them to come.

♦ What did Jesus call out to the people in John 7:37?

♦ According to Revelation 21:6, what does Jesus say that he will freely give?

♦ Who is invited to come and drink, according to Revelation 22:17?

Conclusion

Do you remember the woman at the well? Jesus made an outlandish claim to her: "Whoever drinks of this water will thirst again, but whoever drinks of the water that I shall give him will never thirst. But the water that I shall give him will become in him a fountain of water springing up into everlasting life" (John 4:13, 14 NKJV). Like the woman at the well, we recognize our need for living water. We need moisture, a swallow of water, a long, quenching drink. But where do we find water for the soul?

Throughout the course of this study, we will be seeking out four ways in which our thirst can be satisfied. God's work. God's energy. His lordship and his love. You'll find them easy to remember. Just think of the word W-E-L-L.

Receive Christ's Work on the Cross.
The Energy of his Spirit.
His Lordship over your life.
His unending, unfailing Love.

Drink deeply and often. And out of you will flow rivers of living water.

Prayer of the Thirsty

This is the prayer of the thirsty soul who has turned to the only Source of living water. It is the prayer of a heart ready to receive—to drink deeply from the well of God's work, energy, lordship, and love. Take the time each day to pray this prayer aloud. Learn what a vast resource God has made available to you. Make it the cry of your heart.

> *Lord, I come thirsty. I come to drink, to receive. I receive Your work on the cross and in Your resurrection. My sins are pardoned and my death is defeated. I receive Your energy. Empowered by Your Holy Spirit, I can do all things through Christ who gives me strength. I receive Your lordship. I belong to You. Nothing comes to me that hasn't passed through You. And I receive Your love. Nothing can separate me from Your love.*

THIS WEEK'S PRAYER REQUESTS

Memory Verse

"Jesus stood and cried out, saying, 'If anyone thirsts, let him come to Me and drink. He who believes in Me, as the Scripture has said, out of his heart will flow rivers of living water.'"

— John 7:37, 38 NKJV

Suggested Reading for this Week from *Come Thirsty* by Max Lucado:

- Read the Introduction of *Come Thirsty*: "Meaghan"—As you read through "Meaghan," her story will sound strangely familiar. As this introduction unfolds, we discover a young woman who is thirsting for something real.

- Read Chapter 1 of *Come Thirsty*: "The Dehydrated Heart"—Unless we are drinking deeply at the well of God's supply, our hearts become dehydrated—dry, depleted, parched, and weak.

W-E-L-L

Receive Christ's Work on the cross.

⁓ ᴄ WEEK 2 ᴄ ⁓

GRACE BLOCKERS

*"For by grace you have been
saved through faith, and that not
of yourselves; it is the gift of God."*

—Ephesians 2:8 NKJV

Introduction

Your heart is thirsty, so you make your way to
the water fountain of God's grace for a drink. You've
been there before. It's an abundant source of living
water. Crystal clear streams forever flowing into shining
pools at the foot of the throne. Drinking deeply of
God's grace is just what your soul needs right now.
The recollection of its plentiful supply and satisfying
coolness quickens your step. But as you draw near,
you're astonished to find a handmade sign taped
crookedly to the fountain's edge. "No swallowing,
please. Taste, but don't drink." You look around,
wondering if this can be a prank—someone's idea of
a joke. Shrugging, you dip into the cooling water, but

only enough to wet your lips. And so you turn back, your disappointed heart still longing for refreshment.

Does such a sign sound absurd? It should. But that's what happens when people try to place limitations on God's grace. They block up the fountain of grace. They monitor our every sip. They stand by with arms folded, directing us to swish and spit, when all the while God intended us to drink, and drink deeply.

1. Let's start with grace—unmerited favor. What does the New Testament teach us about the grace of God that is extended toward us? Match up these truths with the verse in which it can be found.

____ 1 Corinthians 15:10   a. Because of grace, we have everlasting hope.

____ Ephesians 1:6   b. By grace we have been made heirs.

____ Colossians 3:16   c. Sing to the Lord with grace in your hearts.

____ Colossians 4:6   d. Grace was ours even before time began.

____ 2 Thessalonians 2:16   e. By grace, we are accepted in the Beloved.

___ 2 Timothy 1:9   f. Be good stewards
of God's manifold
grace.

___ 2 Timothy 2:1   g. We can approach
the throne of grace
boldly.

___ Titus 3:7   h. Let your speech
always be with
grace.

___ Hebrews 4:16   i. Rest your hope
fully upon grace.

___ 1 Peter 1:13   j. Be strong in grace.

___ 1 Peter 4:10   k. By the grace of
God, I am what
I am.

2. What good is grace if you don't let it go deep?
Look at these verses, and more specifically, look
at the words used to describe God's grace.

Romans 3:24: "Being justified _____ by His grace" (NKJV).

Romans 5:20: "Where sin abounded, grace

_____ _____

_____" (NKJV).

2 Corinthians 9:8: "God is able to make all __

_____ _____ toward you, that you, always having _____ _____

_____ in _____ things, may have an

_____ for _____

good work" (NKJV).

Ephesians 2:7: "That in the ages to come He might show the _____ riches of His grace in His kindness toward us in Christ Jesus" (NKJV).

1 Timothy 1:14: "The grace of our Lord was

_____ _____"

(NKJV).

Abundant. Free. Sufficient. Rich. God's grace is excessive—more plentiful than our need. In fact, it is all we need. But there were those in the early church who tried to staunch the flow of grace. They wanted to impose limits. They tried to control it. They molded it to fit into their traditions. They redefined it to suit their purposes. And they deceived God's people by touting it as truth.

3. What new rules did some try to impose on Gentile believers, according to Acts 15:1?

4. The Galatian church also ran into problems. Paul was astonished by how far off track they had been lured.
Galatians 1:6, 7—"God, by his grace through Christ, called you to become his people. So I am _____ that you are _____ _____ _____ so quickly and believing something _____ than the _____ _____. Really, there is _____ _____ Good News. But some people are _____ you; they want to _____ the Good News of Christ" (NCV).

Legalism. Grace blockage. It's thinking that your Heavenly Father might let you in the gate, but you've got to earn your place at the table. God makes the down payment on your redemption, but you still have to pay the monthly installments. Heaven gives the boat, but you've got to row it if you ever want to see the other shore. They don't allow you to receive God's work. They try to tell you to earn it.

    5. Grace, by definition, excludes our efforts to earn it. Why does Paul say that grace cannot come by works in Romans 11:6?

Grace by faith is one of Paul's most adamant themes. "People cannot do any work that will make them right with God. So they must trust in him, who makes even evil people right in his sight. Then God accepts their faith, and that makes them right with him" (Rom. 4:5 NCV). One way, and only one. By grace, through faith.

6. Why does Ephesians 2:8, 9 say we have no reason to boast over our place in God's family?

Beware when faith changes from grace receiving to law keeping. Take care when salvation is limited to those who can meet the standards and accomplish the tasks. We cannot earn God's grace. We can only receive God's work. That's when our hearts are able to drink deeply from the well of living water.

7. What is the work that we must receive? Christ's work on the Cross. Or to ask the question as we find it in Scripture, "What must I do to be saved?" (Acts 16:30 NKJV).

♦ How is this question answered in Acts 16:31?

♦ According to 2 Corinthians 5:21, how were we freed from sin?

♦ What did Jesus say we must believe in order to be saved, according to John 8:24?

> "GOD REFUSES TO COMPROMISE THE SPIRITUAL PURITY OF HEAVEN. HEREIN LIES THE AWFUL FRUIT OF SIN. LEAD A GODLESS LIFE AND EXPECT A GODLESS ETERNITY. SPEND A LIFE TELLING GOD TO LEAVE YOU ALONE AND HE WILL."

And so our sins are forgiven. Christ responded to universal sin with a universal sacrifice, taking on the sins of the entire world. This is Christ's work *for* you. But the salvation we receive doesn't stop there. Jesus not only took your place on the Cross, he takes His place in your heart. This is Christ's work *in* you.

8. How does Paul describe those who have drunk deeply at the well of grace?

● What does Romans 4:7 say about those who have received Christ's work *for* us?

● How has our life been changed by Christ's work *in* us, according to Romans 6:6?

You will occasionally sin. And when you do, remember: sin may touch, but cannot claim you. Christ is in you! Trust his work *for* you. He took your place on the Cross. And trust his work *in* you. Your heart is his home, and his home is sin free.

"SIN MAY, AND WILL, TOUCH YOU, DISCOURAGE YOU, DISTRACT YOU, BUT IT CANNOT CONDEMN YOU."

9. There are many voices telling you who you should be and what you should do. Which ones have you heard lately? Which ones have you been listening to?

❑ You don't do enough.

❑ You don't fit in.

❑ You don't meet the standard.

❑ You ought to know better.

❑ You've made too many mistakes.

❑ You've got to try harder.

❑ You're not doing it the right way.

❑ You're not making a difference.

❑ You're not smart enough.

❑ You need to snap out of it.

❑ What would people think?

❑ What were you thinking?

❑ It's your own fault.

❑ It's too late.

❑ I told you so.

You are who *God* says you are. Grace defines you. People may have opinions, but they hold no clout. Only God does. His is the only opinion that matters, and according to him, you are his. Period.

10. Who does God say you are? What does Ephesians 2:10 say?

Conclusion

Receive God's work. Drink deeply from his well of grace. Your deeds don't save you. And your deeds don't keep you saved. God does. Can I urge you to trust this truth? Let your constant prayer be this: "Lord, I receive Your work. My sins are pardoned." Trust the work of God for you. Then trust the presence of Christ in you. Take frequent, refreshing drinks from his well of grace. You need regular reminders that you are not fatally afflicted! Don't live like you are.

Prayer of the Thirsty

Return to this prayer, paying close attention to the heartfelt meaning in the first few sentences. You came to God thirsty, and he answers you with the satisfying work of grace. Savor Christ's work for you and in you. Let the truth of salvation refresh your soul.

Lord, I come thirsty. I come to drink, to receive. I receive Your work on the cross and in Your resurrection. My sins are pardoned and my death is defeated. I receive Your energy. Empowered by Your Holy Spirit, I can do all things through Christ who gives me strength. I receive Your lordship. I belong to You. Nothing comes to me that hasn't passed through You. And I receive Your love. Nothing can separate me from Your love.

THIS WEEK'S PRAYER REQUESTS

Memory Verse

*"For by grace you have been saved
through faith, and that not of
yourselves; it is the gift of God, not
of works, lest anyone should boast.
For we are His workmanship, created
in Christ Jesus for good works,
which God prepared beforehand
that we should walk in them."*

—Ephesians 2:8–10 NKJV

Suggested Reading for this Week from *Come Thirsty* by Max Lucado:

- Chapter 2: "Sin Vaccination"—We were all born with a terminal disease—hopelessly infected by sin. See how God made a way for us to live disease free.

- Chapter 3: "When Grace Goes Deep"— Grace is a gift of God. Take a look at what happens when you try to put conditions on the grace of God. Grace is what defines us.

- Chapter 4: "When Death Becomes Birth"— Don't allow the dread of death to take away your joy of living.

- Chapter 5: "With Heart Headed Home"—We live, caught between what is and what will be. Our hearts are longing for heaven, and every day that passes brings us closer to home.

W-E-L-L

Receive the Energy of his Spirit.

WEEK 3

REDEFINING PRAYER

*"'Not by might nor by
power, but by My Spirit,'
says the LORD of hosts."*

—Zechariah 4:6 NKJV

Introduction

We don't like living tired. We were made to flourish
and thrive. But when we do not draw from the well of
God's provision, spiritual thirst leaves us drained, dry,
and drawn. Wobbly-kneed weakness replaces our
vitality. Lackluster living steals away our vibrancy. In
our feebleness, we can be bowled over by the slightest
of disturbances. We cling to wispy willpower, only to
be blown off course by a breeze. We don't like living
tired, but we do. Why? Because we do not ask for
the energy we need. God's energy. Pulsing power.
Supernatural strength. And how do we ask the Father
for this supply? We pray.

1. Jesus promised his disciples that he would
   provide them with the power they needed.

Luke 24:49: "Behold, I send the_____ of My Father upon you; but tarry in the city of Jerusalem until you are _____ with _____ from _____ _____." (NKJV)

Acts 1:8: "You shall_____ _____ when the _____ _____ has _____ _____ you." (NKJV)

When does power come? Thankfully, it's not up to us to generate this energetic life. It is a gift from God, and we need only receive it. Power comes as we allow the God who saved us to change us. Power comes as we allow his Spirit to work in us. Power comes when we get rid of harbored sin through confession. Power comes when we unceasingly seek God's Spirit. And power comes when we pray.

"PRAY IN THE SPIRIT AT ALL TIMES WITH ALL KINDS OF PRAYERS, ASKING FOR EVERYTHING YOU NEED. TO DO THIS YOU MUST ALWAYS BE READY AND NEVER GIVE UP.

—Ephesians 6:18 NCV

(Message Bible)

2. Power comes as you pray. What does Paul urge every believer to do in these verses?

♦ Romans 12:12:

♦ Ephesians 6:18:

♦ 1 Thessalonians 5:17:

"GOD NEVER PROMISES AN ABSENCE OF DISTRESS. BUT HE DOES PROMISE THE ASSURING PRESENCE OF HIS HOLY SPIRIT."

3. David pleads with God to hear him: "Hear me when I call, O God of my righteousness! ... Have mercy on me, and hear my prayer" (Ps. 4:1 NKJV). We need to pray continually and with confidence.

♦ According to Jeremiah 29:12, what does God do?

◊ God hears our prayers, but he also responds. When does Isaiah 65:24 say God answered the call of his people?

◊ Because of Jesus' sacrifice, we can approach God with confidence. How does Hebrews 4:16 tell us to go about finding the help we need?

"THE SPIRIT HELPS US WITH OUR WEAKNESS. WE DO NOT KNOW HOW TO PRAY AS WE SHOULD. BUT THE SPIRIT HIMSELF SPEAKS TO GOD FOR US, EVEN BEGS GOD FOR US WITH DEEP FEELINGS THAT WORDS CANNOT EXPLAIN."

—Romans 8:26 NCV

None of us prays as much as we should, but all of us pray more than we think. In those times when we gasp and sigh and moan. When tears slide silently down our cheeks. When our whole heart aches with need. When the urgency of our situation defies words. Those are the times when the Spirit comes alongside and helps us in our weakness.

4. Just how does the Spirit help us, according to Romans 8:26?

Prayer is commonly earmarked as a spiritual discipline. We admire those saints who dedicate hours to intercession, and we feel guilty because we do not. We all want to spend more time in prayer. But who has time to sit serenely, hands clasped and eyes shut? Do this. Change your definition of prayer. Think of prayers as less an activity *for* God and more an awareness *of* God. Seek to live in uninterrupted awareness. Acknowledge his presence everywhere you go.

5. God promised to be present with those who belong to him. Yet some people dash headlong through life, never seeing or acknowledging God's hand. But those who are aware of God's presence, respond to it.

____ Exodus 33:14   a. In God's presence is fullness of joy.

____ Psalm 16:11   b. The righteous will dwell in God's presence.

____ Psalm 21:6   c. Come into God's presence with singing.

____ Psalm 68:8   d. In God's presence are gladness and blessing.

____ Psalm 100:2   e. In God's presence are times of refreshment.

____ Psalm 140:13   f. In God's presence is rest.

____ Acts 3:19   g. In God's presence the earth itself shakes.

6. David assures us, "The LORD is close to everyone who prays to him, to all who truly pray to him" (Ps. 145:18 NCV).

♦ What encouragement and promise were offered to Joshua in Joshua 1:9?

♦ What promise did Jesus make to his followers in Matthew 28:20?

♦ What dwells in us, according to John 14:17?

♦ What does Deuteronomy 30:14 say we should keep near to us?

"ALL BELIEVERS HAVE GOD IN THEIR HEARTS. BUT NOT ALL BELIEVERS HAVE GIVEN THEIR WHOLE HEART TO GOD."

Often we are called upon to wait awhile for the power we've prayed for. This doesn't mean twiddling

our thumbs or busying ourselves elsewhere. We're
still seeking. We're listening attentively for an answer.
Waiting means watching. If you are waiting on a bus,
you are watching for the bus. If you are waiting on
God, you are watching for God, searching for God,
hoping for God.

7. Knowing that God's presence is with us is a
   good thing. But it is infinitely better to seek
   God out. Go after him. Look for his hand.
   Search for him. Chase after him.

___ Ezra 7:10   a. Those who seek the
                          Lord will praise Him.

___ Psalm 9:10   b. Those who seek Him
                          will lack for nothing.

___ Psalm 22:26   c. Seek the Lord's face
                          evermore.

___ Psalm 27:4   d. The LORD does not
                          forsake those who seek
                          Him.

___ Psalm 34:10   e. Those who seek the
                          Lord will rejoice.

___ Psalm 105:3   f. Your heart must be
                          prepared to seek.

___ Psalm 105:4   g. Seek the Lord, seek
                          righteousness, seek
                          humility.

____ Isaiah 55:6 h. Seek the chance to see the beauty of the LORD.

____ Zephaniah 2:3 i. Seek the LORD while He may be found.

8. God is ready to be found by those who seek after him.

♦ What does David say that God is watching for in Psalm 14:2?

♦ What does God ask us to do, and what should our response be, according to Psalm 27:8?

♦ This is no casual game of hide-and-seek. How does Deuteronomy 4:29 say we should seek after God?

"YOU CAN LOOK FOR THE LORD YOUR GOD, AND YOU WILL FIND HIM IF YOU LOOK FOR HIM WITH YOUR WHOLE BEING."

—Deuteronomy 4:29 NCV

The Spirit fills as prayers flow. Desire to be filled with strength? Of course you do. Then pray, "Lord, I receive Your energy. Empowered by Your Holy Spirit, I can do all things through Christ who gives me strength."

9. It's not up to us. We can't depend on our own limited resources. Strength comes from God. Pray for his energy, for his power, for his Spirit.

"'Not by _____ (no amount of stamina, oomph or grit will help) nor by _____, (don't rely on independence, authority, or willpower) but by _____ _____,' (spiritual strength is the power we need) says the LORD of hosts." (Zech. 4:6 NKJV)

10. When our heart thirsts for energy, we need only turn to the only Source of living water for the strength we need. "But You, O LORD, do not be far from Me; O My Strength, hasten to help Me!" (Ps. 22:19 NKJV).

Exodus 15:2: "The LORD is my _____ _____"

2 Samuel 22:33: "God is my _____ _____"

Psalm 73:26: "God is the _____ _____"

Psalm 20:6: "He will answer with _____ _____"

Conclusion

What would life be like if we never learned about the energy available to us through the Holy Spirit? Would you live under the assumption that your spiritual walk was all up to you? Would you have to rely on your own strength, ingenuity, and willpower to please God? All the responsibility for your spiritual state would rest on your own shoulders. Fighting to stay spiritually afloat would burn you out. Your efforts toward righteous living would exhaust you. What kind of life would you lead? A parched and prayerless one.

But what happens to the soul who seeks after God. What happens to the one who taps into God's vast resources? What happens to the person who believes in the work of the Spirit? Really believes. Is there a difference? Yes, indeed! Shoulders lift as the buckling weight of self-salvation drops away. Knees bend as they discover the power of the praying Spirit. And best of all, there abides a quiet confidence that comes from knowing it's not up to you.

Prayer of the Thirsty

Lift up this prayer once again to the Lord. You have learned what it means to receive his work. Now you are reaching out to him, asking to receive his energy. As you repeat this prayer again and again through the week ahead, remember where your strength comes from, and learn to rely on it.

Lord, I come thirsty. I come to drink, to receive. I receive Your work on the Cross and in your resurrection. My sins are pardoned and my death is defeated. I receive Your energy. Empowered by Your Holy Spirit, I can do all things through Christ who gives me strength. I receive Your lordship. I belong to You. Nothing comes to me that hasn't passed through You. And I receive Your love. Nothing can separate me from Your love.

This Week's Prayer Requests

Memory Verse

*"Let us therefore come boldly
to the throne of grace, that we
may obtain mercy and find
grace to help in time of need."*

—Hebrews 4:16 NKJV

Suggested Reading for this Week from *Come Thirsty* by Max Lucado:

- Chapter 6: "Hope for Tuckered Town"— Some of us try to live our Christian lives completely in our own power. God offers hope for us when the effort wears us down.
- Chapter 7: "Waiting for Power"—Before we move forward, sometimes God asks us to wait ... and pray.
- Chapter 8: "God's Body Glove"—The Holy Spirit works with us and through us, hand in glove.
- Chapter 9: "It's Not Up to You"—God paid too high a price for you to leave you unguarded. The Holy Spirit reminds us of our place in God's heart and comes to our aid in times of weakness.

W-E-L-L

Receive his Lordship over your life.

~ WEEK 4 ~

CHOOSING PEACE

*"You cannot add any time to
your life by worrying about it."*

—Matthew 6:27 NCV

Introduction

What's to worry about? Plenty. We worry about
big stuff and little stuff, things we did and things we're
going to do, things we're responsible for and things
we have no control over. Wouldn't you love to stop
worrying? Could you use a strong shelter from life's
harsh elements? God offers you just that. The
possibility of a worry-free life. Not just less worry,
but no worry.

You might be thinking, "Are you kidding?" Worry
can be hard to shake. It comes so naturally to most of
us. But Jesus wasn't kidding when he told us not to
worry in this world. In fact, there are two words that
summarize his opinion of worry: irrelevant and
irreverent.

1. We worry every day about everyday things.
   Jesus knew this, and so he addressed our worries
   in the Gospels. What do each of these verses
   say we tend to worry over?

   ◆ Psalm 37:1:

   ◆ Psalm 37:7:

   ◆ Matthew 6:25:

   ◆ Matthew 6:28:

   ◆ Matthew 6:31:

   ◆ Matthew 6:34:

2. David advises, "Do not fret—it only causes
   harm" (Ps. 37:8 NKJV). What is the use of
   worrying, according to Jesus in Matthew 6:27?

Worry betrays a fragile faith. In essence we're saying we doubt God's ability to take care of us. We aren't so sure he knows what he's doing. We're not convinced that he has our best interests in mind. And so we're reluctant to give over control—to accept God's lordship over our lives. It's subtle, even unintentional at times. But when we worry, we doubt God.

3. How could we possibly think that an all-powerful God might lose his grip? Or that an all-knowing God might make a mistake? Scripture is very clear. God *is* in control.

Psalm 115:3: "Our God is in heaven. He _____ what he _____." (NCV)

Isaiah 43:13: "I have _____ been _____....When I do something, no one can _____ it." (NCV)

Isaiah 46:10: "When I _____ something, it _____. What I _____ to do, I _____ do." (NCV)

Lamentations 3:37: "Nobody can _____ and have it happen _____ the Lord _____ it." (NCV)

Acts 2:23: "This was God's _____ which he had made _____ _____; he knew all this would _____." (NCV)

Acts 17:25: "This God is the One who gives life, breath, and everything else to people. He does not need any _____ from them; he has _____ he _____." (NCV)

Ephesians 1:11: "In Christ we were chosen to be God's people, because from the very beginning God had _____ this in keeping with his _____. And he is the One who makes everything _____ with what he _____ and _____." (NCV)

According to the Bible, God is worthy of all the glory he receives. He does as he pleases. Who are we to question it? But we often have trouble accepting this because it goes against our own agendas. We pursue the wrong priority. We want good health, good income, a good night's rest, and a good retirement. Our priority is *we*. God's priority, however, is God.

4. God always knows what is best. We don't always like it, but what else can we say?
   ♦ What does Isaiah 45:7 say God is able to do?

♦ What does Solomon urge us to remember in Ecclesiastes 7:14?

♦ What is God able to command according to Lamentations 3:38?

♦ And according to Isaiah 48:10, 11, why does God do these things?

Worry comes from the Greek word that means "to divide the mind." Anxiety splits us right down the middle, creating a double-minded thinker. Perception is divided, distorting our vision. Strength is divided, wasting our energy.

How can we stop doing so? Paul offers a two-pronged answer: "Do not worry about anything, but pray and ask God for everything you need, always giving thanks" (Phil. 4:6 NCV). Our part in staving off worry includes prayer and gratitude.

5. The first strategy to purge the worry out of your life is prayer. Paul says not to worry, but to pray.

   ♦ What does Luke 18:1 say we should always do, and never do?

   ♦ Who should pray, according to James 5:13?

   ♦ How does Paul say we should pray in Colossians 4:2?

6. The second thing Paul urges is thanksgiving. Worry has a hard time taking hold of a heart that is thanking God for his faithfulness in the past. Why should we be thankful, according to Psalm 107:8?

Our part is prayer and thanksgiving. What's God's part? Peace. Believing prayer ushers in God's peace. Not a random, nebulous, earthly peace, but his peace. God does not battle anxiety. God enjoys perfect peace because God enjoys perfect power. And he offers his peace to you.

7. Peace

____ Numbers 6:26   a. May the Lord of peace give you peace always.

____ Luke 1:79   b. May the LORD watch over you and give you peace.

____ John 14:27   c. Peace I leave with you; My peace I give to you.

____ Romans 3:17   d. Only those who belong to God will find peace.

____ 2 Thessalonians 3:16   e. God will guide our feet into the way of peace.

"JESUS USED THIS STORY TO TEACH HIS FOLLOWERS THAT THEY SHOULD ALWAYS PRAY AND NEVER LOSE HOPE."

—Luke 18:1 NCV

Peace is precious because there is no substitute. Lust may masquerade as love, and happiness might try to stand in for joy, but there is no mimic for peace.

8. What is the peace of God able to do, according to Philippians 4:7?

"DON'T LOOK FORWARD IN FEAR, LOOK BACKWARD IN APPRECIATION. GOD'S PROOF IS GOD'S PAST. FORGETFULNESS SIRES FEARFULNESS, BUT A GOOD MEMORY MAKES FOR A GOOD HEART."

9. If we want a heart filled with peace rather than worry, what must we let peace do, according to Colossians 3:15?

Letting go of worries means letting God know that you trust him. We need to let peace rule in our hearts. Sure, worries and fears might try to usurp the throne, but the peace that rules is also the peace that guards.

10. What does 1 Peter 5:7 say that we should do with all our worries and cares?

"Cast." Not place, lay, or occasionally offer. Strong verb there. Peter enlists the same verb Gospel writers used to describe the way Jesus treated demons. "He cast them out." An authoritative hand on the collar, another on the belt, and a "Don't come back." Do the same with your fears. Get serious with them. Immediately cast them upon God.

Conclusion

God can lead you into a worry-free world. Amazing, but true. So be quick to pray. Focus less on the problems ahead and more on the victories behind. Trust his sovereignty. Let him be the Lord. You do your part and God will do his. He will guard your heart with his peace…a peace that passes understanding.

Prayer of the Thirsty

We come once again to the prayer of the thirsty.

Lord, I come thirsty. I come to drink, to receive. I receive Your work on the cross and in Your resurrection. My sins are pardoned and my death is defeated. I receive Your energy. Empowered by Your Holy Spirit, I can do all things through Christ who gives me strength. I receive Your lordship. I belong to You. Nothing comes to me that hasn't passed through You. And I receive Your love. Nothing can separate me from Your love.

THIS WEEK'S PRAYER REQUESTS

Memory Verse

*"Be anxious for nothing, but
in everything by prayer and
supplication, with thanksgiving,
let your requests be made known
to God; and the peace of God,
which surpasses all understanding,
will guard your hearts and
minds through Christ Jesus."*

—Philippians 4:6, 7 NKJV

Suggested Reading for this Week from *Come Thirsty* by Max Lucado:

- Chapter 10: "In God We (Nearly) Trust"—We know that God knows what's best. We know that we don't. We also know that God cares, so we can trust him.
- Chapter 11: "Worry? You Don't Have To"—Worry changes nothing, and only shows that we aren't trusting God to do as he promised.
- Chapter 12: "Angels Watching Over You"—When you accept God's lordship in your life, you can be assured that many mighty angels will guard you in all your ways.
- Chapter 13: "With God as Your Guardian"—God guards those who turn to him.

W-E-L-L

Receive his unending, unfailing Love.

∼⌒ WEEK 5 ⌒∼

ABIDING IN GOD'S LOVE

"As the Father loved Me,

I also have loved you;

abide in My love."

—John 15:9 NKJV

Introduction

Are you familiar with 1 Corinthians 13? It is often referred to as the "Love Chapter," as it highlights the many facets of pure, godly love. "Love is patient. Love is kind. Love is not boastful or rude." Familiar and reassuring words. Often, we are invited to insert our own name into the wording of the chapter, personalizing it. "Jane is not easily provoked. Bill thinks no evil. Amanda bears all things." But have you ever considered that all these admirable qualities also apply to God in his love for us? When we say that God loves us, we can rest assured that God's love for us is patient. His love for us is kind. In his great love for us, he bears with us and rejoices when we choose good things. Love never fails, and neither does God.

1. When you want to learn about love, you must start at the source. What are the beloved disciple's familiar words in 1 John 4:7, 8?

"_____, let us _____ one another, for _____ is of God; and everyone who _____ is born of God and knows God. He who does not _____ does not know God, for _____ _____ _____." (1 John 4:7, 8 NKJV)

2. What does God's love for us look like?

◆ How did God demonstrate his love for us, according to Romans 5:8?

◆ When we are saved, what does God do, according to Romans 5:5?

◆ Because of God's great love for us, what does he call us, according to 1 John 3:1?

God pours out his love on his children. It's more than bucketfuls. It's more than pond-fuls. It's more than lake-fuls. It's more than ocean-fuls. We're drenched in it. Saturated by it. Soaked to the skin. But we cannot be soaked to the very soul if we do not drink it in.

3. How does Jeremiah 31:3 characterize God's love for us?

> *"GOD HAS POURED OUT HIS LOVE TO FILL OUR HEARTS. HE GAVE US HIS LOVE THROUGH THE HOLY SPIRIT, WHOM GOD HAS GIVEN TO US."*
>
> —Romans 5:5 NCV

We already know that God is changeless. "I am the LORD, I do not change" (Mal. 3:6 NKJV). It is not strange to discover that God's love is also changeless. "I have loved you with an everlasting love" (Jer. 31:3 NKJV). Everlasting. Eternal. Never-ending. Always. Ceaseless. Unchangeable. Forever. Ever after.

73

4. In what way does God show his love in Zephaniah 3:17?

"[GOD] LOVES YOU BECAUSE HE IS HE. HE LOVES YOU BECAUSE HE DECIDES TO. SELF-GENERATED, UNCAUSED, AND SPONTANEOUS; HIS CONSTANT-LEVEL LOVE DEPENDS ON HIS CHOICE TO GIVE IT."

5. When you are out on the ocean, you are completely surrounded by water. When you are up in an airplane, there is nothing but clouds and sky. Astronauts who leave our atmosphere are surrounded by star-flecked space. What surrounds believers, according to Ephesians 3:17–19?

Over and around us, as far as the eye can see and beyond. God's love for us is so great, we cannot comprehend its immensity. Paul prays that believers might root themselves into it, drawing strength from it. He wants for us to catch a glimpse of something too big to grasp. It is beyond measure. It is unsearchable in its magnitude. For the love of God is as big as God. After all, God *is* love.

6. The pages of Scripture are filled with love. The love of God. The love of Jesus. The love of believers. Here is just a sampling. Match up the truth with the Bible passage in which it is located.

_____ Psalm 36:7   a. The God of love will be with you.

_____ John 13:34   b. God makes his home with those he loves.

_____ John 14:23   c. Speak the truth in love.

_____ 2 Corinthians 5:14   d. There is comfort in love.

_____ 2 Corinthians 13:11   e. God's lovingkindness is precious to his children.

_____ Ephesians 2:4   f. Keep yourselves in the love of God.

_____ Ephesians 3:19   g. The love of Christ passes all knowledge.

_____ Ephesians 4:15   h. Love one another as I have loved you.

_____ Ephesians 5:2   i. The love of Christ compels us.

_____ Philippians 2:1   j. God directs our hearts into His love.

_____ Colossians 2:2   k. Walk in love.

_____ 2 Thessalonians 3:5   l. Believers are knit together in love.

_____ Jude 1:21   m. God has loved us with a great love.

7. What does Jesus ask us to do in John 15:9, 10?

"As the _____ _____ Me, I also have _____ you; _____ in My _____. If you _____ My _____, you will _____ in My _____, just as I have kept My Father's _____ and _____ in His _____." (NKJV)

To abide in Christ's love is to make his love our home. Settle in. Set up housekeeping. Make ourselves comfortable. When you abide somewhere, you live there. You grow familiar with the surroundings. Jesus abided in God's love. We are invited to abide in Christ's. By doing so, "in this world we are like him" (1 John 4:17 NCV).

> "HE KNOWS YOU BETTER THAN YOU KNOW YOU AND HE HAS REACHED HIS VERDICT. HE LOVES YOU STILL. NO DISCOVERY WILL DISILLUSION HIM, NO REBELLION WILL DISSUADE HIM. HE LOVES YOU WITH AN EVERLASTING LOVE."

8. What is Jesus' idea of abiding, according to John 15:4, 5?

According to Jesus, the branch models his definition of "abiding." The branch must be connected to the vine in order to live, grow, and bear fruit. Without the vine, a branch is useless. It can do nothing. We need to hang on to Christ as a branch clutches the vine. If we don't, we go thirsty.

9. With a God who draws us with lovingkindness and promises everlasting love, how can we resist? What is the response of believers to God's outpouring, according to 1 John 4:19?

"YOU DON'T INFLUENCE GOD'S LOVE. YOU CAN'T IMPACT THE TREE-NESS OF A TREE, THE SKY-NESS OF THE SKY, OR THE ROCK-NESS OF A ROCK. NOR CAN YOU AFFECT THE LOVE OF GOD."

We cannot earn God's love. We cannot barter for it. We cannot plead with God to love us. It would be useless to try, because he already does. He loved us first. All we can do is respond to God's love, abide in his love, love in return.

10. What question does Paul raise in Romans 8:35? And what resounding promise is the answer, found in verses 38 and 39?

Nothing can separate us from the love of God. Paul is convinced of this! "I am convinced that nothing can ever separate us from His love." He uses the perfect tense, implying: "I have become and I remain convinced." This is no passing idea or fluffy thought, but rather a deeply rooted conviction. Paul is absolutely sure. You can be, too!

Conclusion

Nothing can shake your Heavenly Father's love for you. God knows your entire story, from first word to final breath, and with clear assessment declares, "You are mine." Step to the well of his love and drink up. Occasional drinks won't bedew the evaporated heart. Ceaseless swallows will. Take your fill. The supply is boundless, everlasting.

Prayer of the Thirsty

We return to this prayer of the thirsty soul. It is the prayer of a heart ready to receive God's love. Unconditional, unreserved, immeasurable love. Take the time each day to pray this prayer aloud. Let it recall to your heart and mind just how precious you are to the Father.

Lord, I come thirsty. I come to drink, to receive. I receive Your work on the Cross and in Your resurrection. My sins are pardoned and my death is defeated. I receive Your energy. Empowered by Your Holy Spirit, I can do all things through Christ who gives me strength. I receive Your lordship. I belong to You. Nothing comes to me that hasn't passed through You. And I receive Your love. Nothing can separate me from Your love.

THIS WEEK'S PRAYER REQUESTS

Memory Verse

"Yes, I am sure that neither death, nor life, nor angels, nor ruling spirits, nothing now, nothing in the future, no powers, nothing above us, nothing below us, nor anything else in the whole world will ever be able to separate us from the love of God that is in Christ Jesus our Lord."

—Romans 8:38, 39 NCV

Suggested Reading for this Week from *Come Thirsty* by Max Lucado:

- Chapter 14: "Going Deep"—Plunge into the depths of the limitless love of God.

- Chapter 15: "Have You Heard the Clanging Door?"—Some fear they've gone too far, done too much, wandered too long to be worthy of God's love. But the God who knows everything about you loves you still.

- Chapter 16: "Fearlessly Facing Eternity"— God knows our imperfections, yet has chosen us. We need never fear God's judgment. Trust his love.

- Chapter 17: "If God Wrote You a Letter"—If God sent you a personal letter, it might read something like this.

NOTES

W-E-L-L

Receive Christ's Work on the cross.

Receive the Energy of his Spirit.

Receive his Lordship over your life.

Receive his unending, unfailing Love.

～⌒ Week 6 ⌒～

If God Wrote You
a Letter

"The Lord will guide you
continually, and satisfy your soul
in drought, and strengthen your
bones; you shall be like a watered
garden, and like a spring of
water, whose waters do not fail."

—Isaiah 58:11 NKJV

Introduction

The final chapter of Max's *Come Thirsty* asks you to pause and consider, what if God wrote you a letter? In a way, he did. The Scriptures stand as a lengthy piece of correspondence from the Father's heart to his people. Max takes the time to condense God's message in a way that speaks to our thirsting hearts. Let's take a more careful look at the promises this letter holds.

We'll take the letter in small sections. Take your time. Meditate over each of these verses. Consider what God is telling you about himself. What does he want you to know? What is he promising you? Then give yourself time to respond. What would happen if this was a dialogue? What would be your reply? Consider what you would like to tell God in return.

If God Wrote You a Letter

Are you thirsty? Come and drink. I am One who comforts you. I bought you. I complete you. I delight in you and claim you as my own, rejoicing over you as a bridegroom rejoices over his bride. I will never fail nor forsake you.

____ Isaiah 55:1	a. You were bought at a price.
____ Isaiah 51:12	b. The LORD delights in you and rejoices over you.
____ 1 Corinthians 6:20	c. I am he who comforts you.
____ Colossians 2:10	d. He will never leave you nor forsake you.
____ Isaiah 62:4, 5	e. Everyone who thirsts, come to the waters.

____ Hebrews 13:5 f. You are complete in him.

Accept My Work

I know your manifold transgressions and your mighty sins, yet my grace is sufficient for you. I have cast all your sins behind my back, trampled them under my feet, and thrown them into the depths of the ocean! Your sins have been washed away, swept away like the morning mists, scattered like the clouds. O return to me, for I have paid the price to set you free.

____ Amos 5:12 a. God has cast all your sins behind his back.

____ 2 Corinthians 12:9 b. You have been washed, sanctified, justified.

____ Isaiah 38:17 c. Our transgressions have been blotted out.

____ Micah 7:19 d. He knows all about your transgressions.

____ 1 Corinthians 6:11 e. All our sins have been cast into the sea.

____ Isaiah 44:22   f. God's grace is
sufficient.

Your death is swallowed up in victory. I disarmed the evil rulers and authorities and broke the power of the devil, who had the power of death. Blessed are those who die in the Lord. Your citizenship is in heaven. Come, inherit the kingdom prepared for you where I will remove all of your sorrows, and there will be no more death or sorrow or crying or pain.

____ 1 Corinthians 15:54   a. Blessed are those who die in the Lord.

____ Colossians 2:15   b. Principalities and powers have been disarmed.

____ Hebrews 2:14   c. We shall inherit a kingdom prepared for us.

____ Revelation 14:13   d. Every tear shall be wiped away.

____ Philippians 3:20   e. Death is swallowed up in victory.

____ Matthew 25:34   f. He has destroyed the devil's power over death.

___ Revelation 21:4   g. Our citizenship is in heaven.

Rely on My Energy

You are worried and troubled about many things; trust me with all your heart.

I know how to rescue godly people from their trials. My Spirit helps you in your distress. Let me strengthen you with my glorious power. I did not spare my Son but gave him up for you. Won't I give you everything else? March on, dear soul, with courage! Never give up. I will help you. I will uphold you.

___ Luke 10:41   a. We are strengthened by God's glorious power.

___ Proverbs 3:5   b. We do not lose heart.

___ 2 Peter 2:9   c. God gives us freely of all the things we need.

___ Romans 8:26   d. The LORD knows how to deliver the godly.

___ Colossians 1:11   e. You are worried and troubled about many things.

___ Romans 8:32   f. March on in strength.

_____ Judges 5:21   g. The Spirit helps us in our weaknesses.

_____ 2 Corinthians 4:1   h. God will help you. he will uphold you.

_____ Isaiah 41:10   i. Trust in the LORD with all your heart.

Trust My Lordship

Trust in me always. I am the eternal Rock, your Shepherd, the Guardian of your soul. When you go through deep waters and great trouble, I will be with you. When you go through rivers of difficulty, you will not drown! When you walk through the fire of oppression, you will not be burned up; the flames will not consume you.

_____ Isaiah 26:3, 4   a. He is the Shepherd and Overseer of our souls.

_____ 1 Peter 2:25   b. God will keep us in perfect peace.

_____ Isaiah 43:2   c. He will be with you through everything.

*So don't worry. I never tire or sleep. I stand beside you.
The angel of the LORD encamps around you. I hide you
in the shelter of my presence. I will go ahead of you
directing your steps and delighting in every detail of your
life. If you stumble, you will not fall, for I hold you by
the hand. I will guide you along the best pathway for
your life. Wars will break out near and far, but don't
panic. I have overcome the world. Don't worry about
anything; instead, pray about everything. I surround you
with a shield of love.*

____ Matthew 6:34

a. Be strong, don't be
afraid, God goes
with you.

____ Psalm 121:3

b. He holds our hand
and leads us.

____ Psalm 34:7

c. He who keeps you
will not slumber.

____ Psalm 31:20

d. He has overcome
the world.

____ Deuteronomy 31:6

e. Don't fear when you
hear rumors of war.

____ Psalm 37:23, 24

f. The angel of the
LORD encamps
around God's
people.

____ Psalm 139:10

g. The LORD will bless
the righteous.

____ Matthew 24:6

____ John 16:33

____ Philippians 4:6

____ Psalm 5:12

h. The LORD orders our steps and upholds us.

i. Do not worry about tomorrow.

j. God will hide us and keep us secretly.

k. Be anxious for nothing, but pray.

I will make you fruitful in the land of suffering, trading beauty for ashes, joy for mourning, praise for despair. I live with the low-spirited and spirit-crushed. I put a new spirit in you and get you on your feet again. Weeping may go on all night, but joy comes with the morning. If I am for you, who can ever be against you?

____ Genesis 41:52

____ Isaiah 61:1–3

____ Isaiah 57:15

____ Psalm 30:5

____ Romans 8:31

a. God dwells with those who are humble.

b. Joy comes in the morning.

c. God has caused me to be fruitful.

d. If God is for us, who can be against us?

e. God will trade beauty for your ashes.

Receive My Love

I throw my arms around you, lavish attention on you and guard you like the apple of my eye. I rejoice over you with great gladness. My thoughts of you cannot be counted; they outnumber the grains of sand! Nothing can ever separate you from my love. Death can't, and life can't. The angels can't, and the demons can't. Your fears for today, your worries about tomorrow, and even the powers of hell can't keep my love away.

___ Deuteronomy 32:10	a. Nothing can separate us from Christ's love.
___ Zephaniah 3:17	b. God will save you, rejoice over you, quiet you.
___ Psalm 139:17, 18	c. God's thoughts of you are precious.
___ Romans 8:35	d. We are kept as the apple of God's eye.

You sometimes say, "The Lord has deserted us; the Lord has forgotten us." But can a mother forget her nursing child? Can she feel no love for a child she has borne? But even if that were possible, I would not forget you! I paid for you with the precious lifeblood of Christ, my sinless, spotless Lamb. No one will snatch you away from me. See, I have written your name on my hand. I call you my friend. Why, the very hairs on your head are all numbered. So, don't be afraid; you are valuable to me.

____ Isaiah 49:14, 15

a. No one can snatch us from His hand.

____ 1 Peter 1:19

b. You're bought with Christ's precious blood.

____ John 10:28

c. Even your hairs are numbered.

____ Isaiah 49:16

d. Christ has called you His friends.

____ John 15:15

e. God cannot forget you.

____ Matthew 10:29–31

f. Your name is inscribed on His hands.

Give me your burdens, I will take care of you. I know how weak you are; that you are made of dust. Give all your worries and cares to me, for I care about what happens to you. Remember, I am at hand. Come to me when you are weary and carry heavy burdens, and I will give you rest. I delight in you; and can be trusted to keep my promise. Come and drink the water of life.

___ Psalm 55:22	a. The Lord is at hand.
___ Psalm 103:13, 14	b. If you thirst, come and drink freely.
___ 1 Peter 5:7	c. The LORD takes pleasure in his people.
___ Philippians 4:5	d. Cast your burden on the LORD; he will sustain you.
___ Matthew 11:28	e. Cast your cares upon Him, He cares for you.
___ Psalm 149:4	f. He who makes us promises is faithful.
___ Hebrews 10:23	g. God remembers that we are made of dust.
___ Revelation 22:17	h. Come to Me and I will give you rest.

Your Maker, Your Father,
God

Conclusion

Promises. Each and every one of those verses you just looked up holds precious and powerful promises. Do you believe them? Then soak in them. Drink them up. And don't stop there. Drink, and keep drinking. Return to them, and to the One who promised them. He holds everything you will ever need.

Prayer of the Thirsty

One more time, pray the prayer of the thirsty.
But don't let it be the last time. You cannot saturate
a dehydrated heart by one quick gulp. Return over
and over to soak. Let this prayer remind you of the
wellspring of life—God's work, his energy, his lordship,
and his love. Yours for the asking.

*Lord, I come thirsty. I come to drink, to receive. I receive
Your work on the Cross and in Your resurrection. My
sins are pardoned and my death is defeated. I receive Your
energy. Empowered by Your Holy Spirit, I can do all
things through Christ who gives me strength. I receive
Your lordship. I belong to You. Nothing comes to me
that hasn't passed through You. And I receive Your love.
Nothing can separate me from Your love.*

THIS WEEK'S PRAYER REQUESTS

Memory Verse

"The LORD will guide you continually, and satisfy your soul in drought, and strengthen your bones; you shall be like a watered garden, and like a spring of water, whose waters do not fail."

—Isaiah 58:11 NKJV

NOTES

NOTES

Notes